SEEING FINGERS

The Story of Louis Braille

*A blind man copies a Braille book on his
Braille typewriter called a brailler.*

Seeing Fingers

THE STORY OF LOUIS BRAILLE

by ETTA DeGERING

illustrated by Emil Weiss

DAVID McKAY COMPANY, Inc.   NEW YORK

To David
who reads with seeing fingers

MANUFACTURED IN THE UNITED STATES OF AMERICA
VAN REES PRESS • NEW YORK
Typography by Charles M. Todd

Foreword

I HAVE SPENT more than ten years becoming acquainted with Louis Braille. During that time I have read all the manuscripts about him available through the associations for the blind, both in France and America; studied books on the Île de France customs and history of his day; learned to read and write the six-dot system of writing for the blind he devised when but a youth. He was fifteen when he completed the simple embossed alphabet, twenty when he considered his project finished, having applied the six-dot key to the various fields of education, and published his method in book form. The system is now known as *Braille* after its inventor.

It was while editor of a Braille magazine for blind

children that I learned to appreciate the world-wide scope of Louis Braille's work. Brailled letters, some in tight little rolls, others folded flat, came through the mail—from David in England, Norman Rock in India, Kwai-Leung Tse, Vietnam, Shoji Kimura, Japan, and from boys and girls and adults all around the globe, as well as the Johns and Sandras of North America—all in the six-dot code.

I have written the story of Louis Braille that you might know him as I have learned to know him. All the main events of the story are documented. The gaps in his boyhood I have filled in after having become acquainted with him as the student and the man, the customs of his day, and the adjustments of other blind children.

And now I leave you with the blind boy of Coupvray, the boy who opened the doors of universities and libraries, and made available the trades and professions of a sighted world to those who read with seeing fingers.

—THE AUTHOR

Boulder, Colorado
April 11, 1962

Contents

CONTENTS

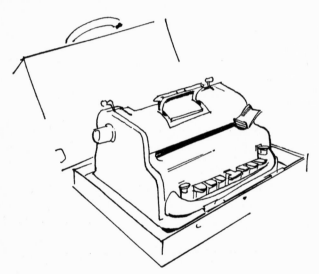

*A Braille writer used by the blind.
It has six keys, each key controls
a dot of the Braille cell.*

ACKNOWLEDGMENTS

My sincere appreciation to:

THE AMERICAN FOUNDATION FOR THE BLIND for making available, 1955, *The Reading Fingers, Life of Louis Braille,* by Jean Roblin, "at present the only authoritative biography of Louis Braille in the English language." Also for the book, *As I Saw It,* by Robert B. Irwin, 1955.

THE ASSOCIATION VALENTIN HAÜY POUR LE BIEN DES AVEUGLES for sending me *La Vie et l'Oeuvre de Louis Braille,* by Pierre Henri, Professeur à l'Institution Nationale des Jeunes Aveugles—the school where Louis Braille was both student and teacher—Presses Universitaires de France, 1952. The book is a historical essay containing valuable quotations from Louis Braille's most intimate biographers, among them his teacher, Dr. Pignier, in *Notice biographique sur trois professeurs anciens élèves de l'Institution des Jeunes Aveugles,* and his friend, Hippolyte Coltat, in *Notice biographique sur L. Braille,* 1853. Also the manuscripts, *Valentin Haüy et son Oeuvre,* by Maurice de la Sizeranne, and *Articles du Journal "La Canne Blanche" sur Valentin Haüy,* by Pierre Henri.

SCHOOL AND SOCIETY, August 2, 1952, for the article, "Louis Braille Centenary," by Godfrey N. Brown (British Student Intern U.N.).

ACKNOWLEDGMENTS

THE CULTURAL DIVISION OF THE FRENCH EMBASSY, New York, for researched information in pamphlet form on the early costumes and holidays of France; also for the vintage song, *"La Vigne au Vin."*

The staff of the CONSULAT GÉNÉRAL DE FRANCE, Denver, Colorado, for help in translating French idiom, and pertinent information on France and its nineteenth-century customs.

And finally, I am especially indebted to Miss Elizabeth Yates, author and teacher, in whose class at the Rocky Mountain Writers' Conference, Boulder, Colorado, *Seeing Fingers* got its start; and to Miss Effie Lee Morris, Children's Specialist, Library for the Blind, New York Public Library, who read the manuscript and offered many helpful suggestions.

—ETTA DEGERING

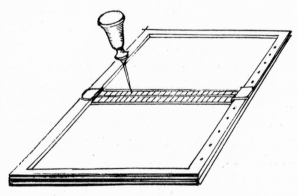

*Slate and writing board of
Louis Braille's day.*

SEEING FINGERS

The Story of Louis Braille

*Blind stereotyper punching plates.
Note three keys under each hand.*

CHAPTER

1

The Harness-maker's Son

IT WAS JANUARY 4, 1809. The ancient clock in the town square of Coupvray—a village that clung hard to the side of a hill twenty-odd miles east of Paris—bonged four in the morning. The sound carried clear and strong in the cold silence but scarcely anyone heard it. The village was still asleep.

All the gray stone houses bordering the narrow cobblestone streets were dark, all that is, except one. Through the lone window of the farmhouse at the foot of steep Touarte Street, on Chemin des Buttes, could be seen the pale yellow glow of candlelight. It was the home of Simon René Braille, the village harness-maker, and his wife Monique. A baby boy had just been born to them.

There were already three children, much older, in the family—Catherine, sixteen and petite like her mother; Simon, a stocky fourteen; and Marie Céline, eleven. They had spent the night with friends in the upper village. Daylight found them hurrying home to welcome the new brother or sister, whichever it might be, and take over the housework and outdoor chores. Simon cautiously opened the low oak door of their farmhouse home. They tiptoed across the well-scrubbed stone floor of the one downstairs room to the bed in the alcove.

Monique opened her tired eyes. *"Bonjour, mes enfants.* (Good morning, my children.) Come meet your new brother."

They stared at the bit of humanity beside their mother. It was so puny, and red, and wrinkled ... "Will he live?" Marie Céline asked.

"We must see that he lives," said Monique. "Tomorrow your father will present him for registration at the mayor's office."

The next morning, in spite of a chill wind that blew down from the hills, bringing rain and snow, the baby was made ready for his registration. Catherine wrapped him in a feather-filled coverlet and placed him in the arms of their father. "Snug as a moth in a cocoon," she said.

Simon René chose his way carefully up the wet cobblestone street. A gust of wind snatched at the coverlet. He held the bundle closer. As he opened the door of the mayor's office, the village clock struck ten.

"*Bonjour*, Monsieur Braille," greeted the deputy mayor who was on duty. "What brings you away from your warm fireside on such a morning? Must be important."

"I have come to register my infant son," said Simon René.

"Ah ha, then it is important, very important."

A grocer and wine-grower were called in as witnesses. The large registry book was taken down from its dusty shelf. The deputy sharpened a quill with his knife and opened the book to the B section. He found the page headed "Simon René Braille and Monique Baron-Braille." Under their names were entered the children born to them. He read the last date of entry.

"Why, Monsieur Braille, it has been eleven years since you registered your last child."

"Yes, Your Honor, it is so. This one shall be the companion of my old age."

The deputy dipped the quill into the inkwell. It made a scratchy, spluttery sound as he wrote out the formal notice of registration. Occasionally he paused for information.

3

"Did you say son or daughter?"

"A son," said Simon René proudly.

Again the quill wrote and paused. "Name?"

"Louis, just Louis," said Simon René, "no middle name."

The page was signed, then blotted with sand. The

4

registry of Louis Braille was complete. He had slept through it all.

The witnesses shook hands with their town craftsman and clapped him on the back. "Congratulations on another man-child!" The wine-grower turned and saluted the bundle on the table. "To Coupvray's future harness-maker!"

"*Non, non,* not this one," said Simon René. "My son Simon will carry on my trade. This one, we have decided, shall study books."

"La, la," said the wine-grower, "a professor, we have witnessed today perchance. 'Tis fine! 'Tis fine!"

Simon René made his way back down the street. The wind slammed the low oak door shut behind him. He stamped the snow off his boots, and carried the baby to its mother in the alcove. "The wind, he blows a terrible gale, wife, like a witch's threat. I trust it holds no bad omen for the child."

"Remember, husband, we no longer believe in witches." But in her heart Monique never could be quite sure—when the wind blew.

The family gathered around to hear the details of the registration. Their father recounted all, from the spluttery quill scratching its way across the page to the jovial wine-grower's suggestion of a professor. The

5

sisters and brother looked at the wrinkled bald mite, now protesting his hunger by a mewing little cry. They laughed; the baby looked so un-professor-like.

"He will grow," stoutly defended Monique. "You will have to swallow your laughs. Wait and see."

Alone, Monique drew her new wee one closer. As she looked into his tiny face, she wondered what secrets life held for him, what the grown man would be. "Maybe," she whispered, "maybe you will be a professor, my little son."

The baby seemed to like what she said. He stopped crying and moved his lips, making a sort of tasting sound, as if the words were good.

Simon René went to sit by the fireplace while he waited for the midday meal. As he comfortably warmed himself, he too fell to musing over the good fortune that was his. . . .

He had inherited this stone farmhouse, the harness shop, and other buildings built more than sixty years ago by his father when he came to Coupvray to ply the trade of harness-making. Besides the large room with alcove downstairs which served as kitchen, living room, and bedroom for the parents, there were two rooms in the garret where the children slept. True,

6

the house was a bit dark for want of more windows, but Monique kept the walls freshly whitewashed, which helped.

He had acquired seven and a half acres of land. It was rich soil and produced well for them. They grew grapes for their year's supply of wine. They raised wheat for their bread, hay for their cow and mare, feed for the poultry, and all the vegetables needed for the soup-pot as well as to share with less fortunate neighbors.

In his trade he had worked hard to earn the coveted title of Master Harness-maker. To do this it was necessary to create and exhibit a first-class piece of work and live up to that quality in all that he put out.

And now he had a complete family, two daughters and two sons. He looked with pride from one to the other.

Catherine capably stirred the soup in the iron pot hung from the chimney hook in the fireplace. The rich smell of onions and the spicy smell of apple pastries baking in the fireplace oven, curled upward together and made him know how hungry he was.

At the far side of the room, Marie Céline was setting the hand-hewn table. On a platter were wedges of cheese and plump figs. She put a large loaf of bread on

7

a cutting board in front of his place, and then drew up the benches where the family would sit. A chair stood at the head of the table for him. When they sat down to eat, he would ask a blessing on the loaf and cut slices for all.

Simon was washing up at the worn old sink. The husky boy was learning fast the harness trade.

And now there was the small Louis . . . Simon René roused himself. "Simon," he called, "go to the wine cellar and bring up a jug of our special wine. It is a time to celebrate! You young folk have a brother, and your mother and I, we have another son."

Three days later Catherine again bundled wee Louis into his cocoon. This time his father took him to the candle-lighted church where he was baptized by the Abbé Pillon. His godparents, Louis François André Michel, a farmer, and Geneviève Boulingre signed the baptismal certificate.

"Our baby is now registered in the department and the church," said Simon René. "Surely, all will be well with him."

CHAPTER

2

"Just a Little Awl"

IT WAS SUMMERTIME and Louis was three and a half years old. No one could call him puny now. He was slim, but muscle-slim. The once bald head was a tangle of blond curls, his blue eyes missed nothing.

In the peasant life of his family Louis found many interesting things for a boy to do. He rode the brown mare while Simon plowed the garden or cultivated the grapes.

At noon every day he walked with Catherine to get water. On the way she told him stories. As the warm dust of the path oozed up between his brown toes, he pretended he was the boy she told about—the boy who fished from a boat in Brittany, or the boy who walked on stilts to herd his sheep in the marsh lands of

Gascony, or that specially privileged boy who cared for the big St. Bernard dogs at the monastery in the mountains. The walks were always too short. He wished the path went on and on, to as far as where the sky met the hills. Then there would be time for many stories.

On wash days he went with his sisters to the old wooden wash-house by the brook. First they boiled the clothes, and then pounded them with paddles on large flat rocks in the running water. Nearby was a high-arched bridge where he liked to watch the oxcarts and hay wagons as they rumbled their creaking way across.

Louis especially liked Thursdays. Thursday was Market Day. All the people from the whole countryside came to town dressed in their gayest clothes on Market Day. They brought vegetables and animals, or whatever they had to sell or trade, to the village square.

Early Thursday morning Marie and Louis helped their mother get the artichokes and cauliflowers ready for market. The brown mare was hitched to the two-wheeled cart and tied to the hitching post while they went to put on their market-day costumes. Marie and Monique wore white blouses, full gathered skirts of bright red and yellow, and black aprons. Last of all they donned the puffy white bonnets trimmed with little pleats and tied them with a bow in the back. The bonnets showed they were from the Île de France countryside. A French woman's bonnet always showed in what part of France she lived. Louis wore long trousers, a short jacket with two rows of shiny brass buttons, and a broad-brimmed hat.

Monique untied the mare from the hitching post and took her place on the seat at the front of the cart. Marie and Louis sat in the back and let their legs hang over.

Their cart joined the procession of other carts— oxcarts, donkey carts, horse carts—most of them with boys and girls dangling their feet. There was no school on Market Day. Mixed in the caravan were folk on foot, men pushing wheelbarrows, and women carrying baskets on their heads or hips, all going to market for a day of trading and fun.

At the village square Louis helped arrange the artichokes and cauliflowers on a table in a neat pile. Other tables were heaped with apples, carrots, cabbages, baskets of eggs, stacks of cheese, yard-long loaves of bread, molds of butter, and crescent-shaped rolls called *croissants*. Tied to stakes by their legs were squealing pigs, clucking hens, bleating goats, hissing geese—all for sale or trade.

Itinerant merchants were there. They displayed cooking pots, bolts of cloth, ribbons, jewelry, and medicines for every kind of pain or ache.

The tradesmen of Coupvray were there. Rope-makers, locksmiths, and weavers, offered their wares for sale. Simon René and Simon had gone early to set up the harness booth.

There were many smells at the market square, some good, some bad. One of the most tempting was that of *petits pains*, little hot rolls, that could be bought for a *sou*

or two. Women munched them as they went from stall
to stall looking for the fattest goose or sweetest butter
or freshest vegetables. Men ate them as they discussed
the price of hay, or complained about the taxes, or waited
for a key to be made at the locksmith's booth. Boys and
girls ate them as they rode on the merry-go-round or
watched the fun-wagon shows. Louis liked *Guignol,* a
Punch and Judy show. When the show was over, the
leading marionette shook hands with each boy and girl.

Market Day always ended with singing and dancing.
And then the long line of carts started home.

Louis spent much of his time in the harness shop
where his father and Simon worked. The shop was in
the dooryard of the house. Every day was magic day
in the harness shop. Louis watched as they slashed
leather with sharp knives, punched holes in it with
pointed awls, and clinched rivets with short-handled
mallets. He watched Simon weave the multi-colored
fringes and make the gay tassels for the finished harnesses. He thought, some day I'll do that.

The scraps of leather were his to play with. He ar-
ranged and rearranged them on the stone doorstep.
Sometimes they were soldiers marching in straight lines,
sometimes they were horses and cows in a pasture.

One day he decided to make a harness out of his pieces of leather. But how could he make a fine harness without tools? He eyed the forbidden row of shiny knives and awls on his father's bench. He would *borrow* just a little awl. With it he tried to punch a hole in a scrap of leather. But the leather was tough and resisting, the awl did not go through. He bent his head closer to see better. He pushed harder. The awl slipped and pierced his eye.

His terrified scream brought his father with a leap over the workbench. His mother and sisters ran from the house. Neighbors came out on their doorsteps.

"Bring a clean cloth and water," said Simon René. An old lady brought lily water which was supposed to stop bleeding. A compress was made, the eye bandaged.

Louis's parents took him to the doctor. But the doctor said, "The eye is very delicate. There is not much that can be done." He read from Dr. Leopold Turck's book, *Popular Medicine:*

TREATMENT FOR EYE INJURIES

Light should be prevented from entering the room, and the eye should be covered with compresses soaked in cold water. Bleeding of

14

*the arm, applications of leeches around the in-
jured eye, diet and a dose of calomel are the
methods usually employed . . . when the eye
has received serious injury.*

Louis seemed too young for the "leech" treatment—
live bloodsuckers attached to the face around the eye
for the purpose of sucking blood and supposedly sucking
out any poisons caused by the accident—but the calomel
and compresses might help. His family would be sure
the compresses were changed often.

But in spite of the family's watchful care, the injured
eye became swollen and inflamed after a few days, and
the other eye began to blur. Louis rubbed it to see
better, but day by day, the trees, the house, his father's
face grew dimmer and dimmer.

One morning Catherine called, "Come, Louis, it's time
to get up. Your breakfast is ready."

"It's dark," said Louis. "It's not morning yet."

"Oh yes, it's morning. Don't you hear the birds singing?"

"Why do they sing when it is dark?" he asked.

Ever after it would be dark for Louis. *He was blind.*

Louis puzzled over what had happened to him. Where
had all the things gone that he used to see? He rubbed

his eyes to take away the dark curtain but it did no good. Day after day he sat like a forlorn, lost little boy on the bench beside the fireplace.

"My poor little one," said Monique, sitting down beside him. She put his favorite toy in his hands, a dog Simon René had made for him from leather.

"What is it?" he asked.

"Why, it's *le petit chien*. Don't you know? The little dog your papa made for you."

But Louis had always seen the toy dog with his eyes. He didn't recognize this "something" his mother had placed in his hands. Small fingers began to explore it. They found the little dog's head, its ears. They slid carefully along its back and discovered the stubby tail, and then the four feet. He smelled its leathery smell and smiled. He had found a new way to *see* the little dog.

Louis slid off the bench and began to *see* other familiar things about the house. He ran his fingers over them inch by inch. He smelled them and sometimes he tasted them.

His family helped him to *see*. When Marie came in with her apron full of eggs, announcing she had found some new hens' nests, Louis asked to see them and edged his way towards her voice. She took the hand he held up to her and guided his fingers over the eggs. Simon held him up to *see* the deserted robin's nest in the tree by the doorstep.

But Louis learned there were some things a blind boy could never see even with this new way of seeing. When Catherine exclaimed, "The moon is new tonight," Louis held up his hand for her to show him the moon. She took him on her lap and explained the moon was too far away to touch, that it was up in the sky, and the sky was the ceiling over the world like a ceiling over a room, only much, much higher. "But I will cut for you a new moon out of paper," she said, "and then you can see how it is curved like papa's grass sickle."

Louis also had to learn there were some things that must not be seen with fingers although they could be reached, such things as the food on other people's plates, the hot soup kettle, and some animals like porcupines and snapping turtles.

At first, as Louis began to walk about, he bumped into things. There were many bruises for mother and sisters to kiss, and many tears to wipe from unseeing eyes. But gradually he found a way to go about and not bump into things. He learned to listen to what the sound waves his walking made, told him. If the sound waves hit against a chair, a wall, or a tree trunk, they made a different sound than when there was only open space in front of him. The waves bounced back against his face and he knew that he had to turn away.

Louis often hummed or made a noise as he walked. The humming made the sound waves stronger, so did tapping with a stick or cane. "When I sing," he said, "I can *see* my way much better." He was learning what bats had always known. As they flew among the trees or chimney tops they kept up a squeaking noise. The sound waves bounced back when they were about to fly into something solid and warned them to change their course. After a time Louis could run and play about the yard, and had few accidents.

People's voices became the faces he knew them by. He rarely made a mistake. When a neighbor called, "*Bonjour*, Louis," he would answer, "*Bonjour*, Madame Boury," or Hurault, or whoever it might be.

As he grew older he learned to recognize the wagons and carts that passed his home. He knew whether they were pulled by horses or oxen and often what they hauled. The quick clop of a team of horses was quite different from the slow plod of the cleft hoofs of a span of oxen. Each vehicle had some sound peculiar to itself, and of course grapes had a different smell from hay or turnips.

Louis surprised Marie one day by saying, "François is driving by. One of his oxen is lame."

"How do you know, Louis?"

"Listen," he said.

Louis didn't like his family to do for him what he could do for himself. He didn't like to hear them say "the poor child" as if he were no longer of much good. Every day he tried to prove to them he was just like other boys, only he did his seeing in a different way.

Louis's problem of adjusting to family life and going about the small world of home was solved. But that was only the beginning. What next? And after that, what?

Often when the children had gone to bed, and the harness-maker and his wife were alone, they talked of their youngest son's future. What would become of him? He could never study books, of that they were sure. Most blind folk they knew or had heard about, made their living by begging. There was one such beggar in Coupvray.

"Louis must never come to that," said Monique.

"*Non, non,* never," agreed Simon René. "I will work harder and you will save more carefully that there may be money for him when we are gone."

CHAPTER

3

New Sounds and a New Friend

I N JUST A FEW DAYS Louis would be five. He was now
old enough, if well-mufflered and mittened, to go
with his father to meet the weekly stagecoach from Paris.
All of the men and boys who possibly could, gathered
on the town square for the once-a-week event. The
driver was their weekly newspaper. He brought the
latest news of the nearby towns . . . young people married, land bought and sold, babies born . . . as well as
the happenings in fashionable Paris. It was a noisy time
with everybody talking at once trying to get the driver's
attention to ask about friends or give him news to pass
on.

But that January day the driver had only one piece
of news. It was from the capital city, and he told it

very slowly to make sure every word was understood. He said, "Napoleon's Grand French Army has met defeat at the river Rhine. The soldiers are retreating in disorder towards Paris."

Louis tried to understand. What did "defeat" mean? He knew it must be terribly serious from the hushed way the grown-ups talked. He had played soldier with his scraps of leather but never "defeat" or "retreat." He would ask his father the meaning of the words on their way home.

The stagecoach drove on toward Meaux, the next town. The group stood silently listening to the horses' hoof beats as they grew fainter and fainter in the distance. Finally someone said, "The Grand French Army defeated? It can't be so."

"There must be some mistake," hopefully suggested another.

Stunned by what they had heard, the men turned towards home without further talk. Louis tugged at his father's coat sleeve and asked questions, but his father didn't seem to hear. He would have to wait until some other time to find out the meaning of the words.

A few days later messengers on fast horses galloped into Coupvray. They stopped at the mayor's office and then spurred their horses on.

Immediately the village drum began calling, "Rat-a-tat-too! Rat-a-tat-too!" People dropped their work and hurried to the village square, where the mayor waited for them.

"Couriers from the Emperor have just ridden through our town," he said. "They not only brought word that the Grand French Army has met defeat at the river Rhine, but also that Napoleon is attempting to reorganize the retreating troops and stop the enemy. He needs supplies. Here is the list expected of Coupvray."

The mayor unfolded a long document and began to read. The people gasped as they heard the list read. It demanded oats and hay, cows and horses, bread and money. . . .

Louis began to understand the meaning of the word "defeat." He cried unconsolably when the brown mare was led away.

The demands kept repeating until well into March. Then there was quiet for a month, the kind of quiet that goes before a storm. At the month's end new sounds were heard in Coupvray, the tramp, tramp of marching soldiers and the rumble of artillery wagons. The Russian grenadiers had come. Napoleon had not been able to stop them. They were marching to Paris, and Coupvray lay in their line of march.

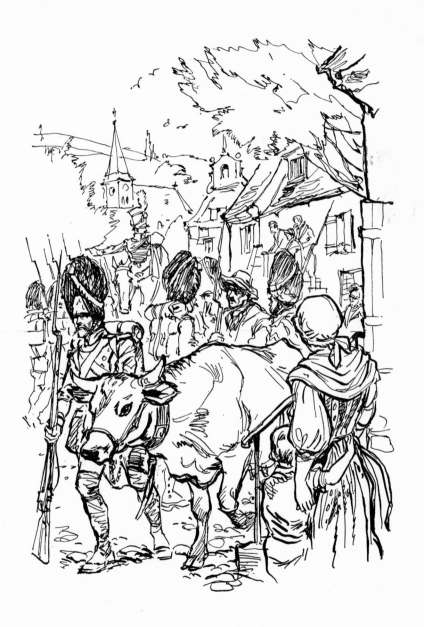

The grenadiers made further demands for wagons, food, and animals. They knocked with gunstocks on the farmhouse door, and argued with Simon René in loud and threatening voices.

Louis hid behind his mother. "What do they say?" he whispered. He could not understand the soldiers' broken French.

"They ask for wine and food, and—and—the cow."

"But we won't give them our cow, will we? Will we, Mama? Please say no, Mama."

Monique put her arms around him as if to shut away the unpleasantness. "It is war, son, we have no choice."

Before the troublous period was over, five armies (French, Russian grenadiers, Bavarian infantry, Russian cuirassiers, and Prussians) had made demands on Coupvray. The people were ground down to poverty. There were no animals, and scarcely any food was left. The Brailles had a small sum of money—the money they had saved for Louis.

"But we cannot stand by and do nothing while our neighbors starve," said Simon René.

"No, we cannot let our neighbors starve," Monique agreed. "We will help them. And then, then we'll start all over again to save for Louis."

There was a knock on the door. They hesitated to

answer. Knocks on the low oak door had brought them so much trouble. But this was not a demanding knock; rather, a gentle query. Simon René opened the door.

"*Bonjour*, my friends! I am the new pastor appointed to Coupvray. Today I have been making calls on the people of my parish. Jacques Palluy is the name."

"Come in, Father, come in. My name is Simon René Braille, and this is my wife, Monique Braille, my daughter Marie, and son Louis." Catherine and Simon had married and were now living in homes of their own. Monique and Marie curtsied low, and Louis remembered, after a nudge from his mother, to bow.

During the pleasant visit that followed, the pastor's attention kept returning to the blind boy. Of course Louis said nothing, as was expected of children, but the Abbé Palluy observed his alert interest in the conversation, the quickness with which he turned his head from one speaker to the other, his knowing smile.

As he was leaving, the abbé asked if the small boy would like to come to his study for a story period the next afternoon.

Would he? Louis's face was answer enough, but his father spoke for him. "Your offer is most kind, Father. Nothing gives the boy more pleasure than a story."

That was the beginning of many days spent with the

25

Abbé Palluy in the old presbytery near the church or under the trees in the garden. It was there Louis learned the first facts of science, about the stars, the habits of animals, how plants grow. He listened to stories of history, and other stories that in turn taught lessons of courage, kindness, and honesty—stories he would always remember.

The trouble-filled year was drawing to a close. Christmas was nearing. Louis and Marie helped their mother bring the crèche from the garret and set it up by the fireplace. The manger was filled with fresh-smelling hay but otherwise left empty until later. The Virgin Mother, the Wise Men, the shepherds, and animals were put in their places. Saints and workers carved from wood were added. Louis was particular that the worker representing harness-makers had a good spot.

Marie made paper angels and suspended them above the scene by thread. Louis climbed on a chair to see them with careful fingers.

"Christmas is good for us," said Simon René. "It makes us think of other things besides our empty barn and empty bins. It has a healing for empty hearts, too. Come, Louis, let us go choose a Yule log."

On Christmas Eve Catherine and Simon and their families came home. They all gathered around the fireplace. Being an uncle made Louis feel grown up. Wine was poured on the Yule log and then it was lit. As it crackled and snapped with flames of bright colors, they sang all the Christmas songs they knew. When the log had burned low, Simon René ended the evening with a special Christmas prayer.

Before going to bed Louis and Marie and their small nephew and niece placed their sabots, wooden shoes, by the fireplace for *le père Noël*, Father Christmas, to fill. The older members of the family went to the midnight service at the church. On their return, while Catherine set the table for *le réveillon*, the traditional late supper of oysters in the Île de France region, Monique reverently placed the doll-figure of the baby Jesus in the waiting manger.

The children were always up first on Christmas morning, eager to see what Father Christmas had left in their sabots, and if the little Jesus was in the manger.

While it was still dark, Louis tiptoed down the stone stairs. His sensitive fingers didn't need a light to see the new mittens and scarf in his sabots. And when those searching fingers touched the baby in the manger he stood very still with the wonder of it all. He was quiet so long that his mother in her alcove bed began to worry. She joined him, and together they kneeled before the manger as did the shepherds in Bethlehem of old.

CHAPTER

4

Swallows and Grape Harvest

MISERY WAS EVERYWHERE in the village of Coupvray the spring after enemy occupation. Children's faces were pinched and pale from too little food, old people's eyes dull from loss of hope. Men, gaunt and hungry, walked the cobblestone streets out of work. An epidemic of smallpox had brought fear to every household. Louis seldom smiled these days.

A committee of citizens met with the marquis, who lived in the old turreted castle on the hill overlooking the village, to see what could be done. The marquis offered work to fifty men. Simon René and others promised a small sum of money to be paid each month into a general fund which would be dispensed by the mayor to those in need. Vaccination was encouraged to stay the smallpox scourge.

It was also decided to re-establish Market Day. Though they had little to sell, it would draw work for the craftsmen of Coupvray from the villages less hurt by the occupation. Besides, there was something about Market Day that lifted spirits and gave courage.

"If we can but hold out," said Simon René, "the good soil of France will repay us."

Already the good soil was showing promise of the truth of his statement. In Monique's garden the points of onions and the blunt heads of early peas were making open cracks in straight rows. The hay meadows were greening, the grapes sending out succulent shoots. Louis reported that the peach tree under which the abbé read to him was in bloom and buzzing with bees.

"But," said he, "Granny Hirault and Monsieur Pigeonot say it's the swallows that bring good luck, and they have not come."

"Louis is right," said Monique. "The villagers are shaking their heads about it. 'There will be no crops,' they say, 'unless the swallows come.'"

"Perhaps they will yet come," suggested Simon René.

"But never have they been so late, husband. Always since we were married our swallows have returned to their nest on the barn rafter many days before this."

Louis hurried to the barn to check. He rarely went

29

there since the mare and cow had been taken away. The old stone building seemed so cold and empty. No longer was there a steamy warmth when he opened the door, no friendly chewing sounds in the cow's stall, no nice horse smell or welcoming nicker from the mare's stall. Today he turned his head toward the rafters and listened. No, there were no bird sounds, either.

Every day now, he sat long hours on the stone wall with his face toward the south, from where his mother said the swallows should come, and listened for the sound of wings. A week went by, a week end—but no swallows.

The villagers said, "The swallows must have been caught in a storm. They will not come now."

Louis still kept sentinel on the stone wall. He would not give up. And then one afternoon, it happened. . . . Suddenly, the air was filled with the shrill calls of swallows.

"Papa! Mama! Marie!" he shouted. "They've come! The swallows have come! Hurry! Hurry!"

The family came running to see the steel blue backs and dusty white breasts of swallows darting here and there and everywhere. "It looks as if heaven had opened and dumped them all out in one tumbling mass," said Simon René.

A pair swept down in front of the Brailles' barn. They wheeled in figure eights. The zigged here and zagged there, putting on a show that was a combination of figure skating and acrobatic stunts. Louis followed their flight by their joyous cries and the snap and whirr of wings. He jumped up and down and clapped his hands.

The swallows flew over the watching family almost brushing their hair with a wing salute. They took a wide turn around the farmhouse and then, as straight as arrows flew into the barn and onto the rafter.

Marie and Louis ran hand in hand to the barn. Now there were bird sounds a-plenty, as Madame Swallow immediately began making ready the saucer-shaped mud and straw nest. In it she would lay five or six eggs, white with splotches of gray and orange.

Monsieur Swallow left the housework to his wife and flew out of the barn to take up his duty as watch on the weathercock.

"Let's go see Monsieur Swallow," said Marie. She made a word-picture of him for Louis. "He looks like a weathercock, himself, with his bill pointing upward into the wind and his long forked tail in the opposite direction."

Monique went back to her work. Now everything

would be all right; the swallows had returned. Simon René turned to the harness shop where a broken tug awaited his mending. Work in his business these days consisted mostly in mending broken straps or bridles, which brought little money. There were no extra *sous* for the saving jug as yet.

It was a looking-up-day when in mid-summer the marquis ordered a new set of double harness complete with fringe and tassels. Marie wove the fringe. Louis begged to make just one of the red tassels. He surprised his family by turning out a nearly perfect one.

"That is good, my son," said Simon René, "very good. Soon you will be ready to try the fringe."

Now they could buy a cow, and a cow meant milk and cheese and butter. The mare's stall would still have to remain empty. But if the grape harvest turned out as good as it gave promise, and with half the hay and oat crops to sell, since there was only one animal to feed, it was just possible the vacant stall could be filled by the next spring. Louis hoped so. He missed the mare so much; he missed her gentle nicker when he went into the barn and the feel of her soft muzzle against his neck and shoulder; he missed the rides on her broad back.

Summer wore on. The sun and the rain seemed to

understand the need and took special care in measuring out their gifts. The good soil did the rest. The oats and hay crops were excellent, and by fall the grapes hung in clusters, large and full.

All other crops were harvested when the owner decided, but not so the grapes. Grape harvest was a community event. The day was set by the Town Council. The drum called the villagers to the town square to hear the formal announcement:

Considering that most of the grapes are ripe and that because of the advanced season there is risk of frost, let us resolve unanimously to begin the grape harvest, Tuesday, October ten, of the year one thousand eight hundred and fifteen.

Catherine came home to help in the grape harvest. The grape baskets were gotten out and mended, the wine barrels and jugs cleaned.

On the morning of the appointed day, each band of pickers, with baskets on their arms, paused outside the vineyard to sing an old vintage song. A leader was chosen to sing the solo parts, the other workers sang the chorus.

Louis's uncle sang the solos in their group. Monique and the older folk clapped as they sang the chorus. Catherine and Marie and the young people danced as they sang since it was a dancing song. Louis and his cousin Jean did all three. They sang and clapped and danced.

FROM VINE TO WINE

La Vigne Au Vin

SOLO:
Let us plant the vine,
There it is, the lovely vine.

Plantons la vigne,
La voilà, la jolie vigne.

CHORUS:
Vine, let us vine, let us
vine the wine,
There it is, the lovely vine
for wine,
There it is, the lovely
vine!

Vigni, vignons, vignons
le vin,
La voilà, la jolie vigne au
vin.
La voilà, la jolie vigne!

SOLO:
From plant to sprout,
There it is, the lovely
sprout.

De plante en pousse,
La voilà, la jolie pousse.

CHORUS:
Sprout, let us sprout, let
us sprout the wine,
There it is, the lovely
sprout for wine.
There it is, the lovely
sprout!

Poussi, poussons, poussons
le vin,
La voilà, la jolie pousse
au vin.
La voilà, la jolie pousse!

34

SWALLOWS AND GRAPE HARVEST

SOLO:

From sprout to flower,
There it is, the lovely
flower.

De pousse en fleur,
La voilà, la jolie fleur.

CHORUS:

Flower, let us flower, let
us flower the wine,
There it is, the lovely
flower for wine.
There it is, the lovely
flower!

Fleuri, fleurons, fleurons
le vin,
La voilà, la jolie fleur au
vin.
La voilà, la jolie fleur!

SOLO:

From flower to grape,
There it is, the lovely
grape.

De fleur en graine,
La voilà, la jolie graine.

CHORUS:

Grape, let us grape, let
us grape the wine,
There it is, the lovely
grape for wine.
There it is, the lovely
grape!

Graini, grainons, grainons
le vin,
La voilà, la jolie graine au
vin.
La voilà, la jolie graine!

The song continued—from green grapes to ripe
grapes, from ripe grapes to the basket, from basket to
barrel, from barrel to glass, from glass to mouth.

After the song the pickers went into the vineyard and began filling baskets with purple, red, or white grapes. Not every cluster was picked. They were careful to leave some for the poor to glean later.

Louis acted as basket and water boy for his family. The long rows of vines made paths easy to follow. In between calls for baskets or water he stayed close to his storytelling sister. Catherine knows so many stories, thought he, and the abbé knows still different ones. Where do all the stories come from?

"How do you know so many stories, Catherine?" he asked.

"Oh, when I was a little girl Grandma Braille told me stories, and then when I went to school I read stories out of books."

"When I go to school I'll read stories out of books, too, won't I?"

There was no reply so he tried again. "There'll be books at school I can read, won't there, Catherine?"

"I—I—I hope so. Louis, I have need of a drink."

He hurried to get the water jug. Catherine sounded choked up—must be the dust.

In the evening after supper everyone, old and young, hired help and visiting friends, gathered on the village square and danced together. They sang the vintage song

and danced to it. They danced other round dances. Louis danced until his feet refused to dance another step. He went to sleep with his head pillowed on his mother's lap, and knew no more until he awoke the next morning on his feather bed in the garret, eager to start another day of grape harvest.

During the cool days of harvest the swallows began to gather in flocks for their autumn migration. The pair on the barn rafter had raised two families. They wheeled around the farmhouse one morning as if taking a last look and then joined a large flock as it winged its way southward. The harvesters called after them.

"*Au revoir* until next May, and don't be late."

"*Au revoir*," echoed Louis. "Don't be late."

CHAPTER
5

"No Books for Blind Boys?"

LOUIS'S seventh year was a very special year, a sort of coming-of-age year. He went through the magic door that left his little-boy-self behind. The magic door was the schoolhouse door. Each morning Cousin Jean called for him. Arm in arm they climbed steep Touarte Street to the school in the upper village.

The girls sat on one side of the room, the boys on the other. The desks and benches were homemade, and seemed to have been built with the same plan in mind their mothers had when making them new coats, "large enough to grow into." It was fun to dangle feet from the back of an oxcart going to market, but quite another thing to dangle them all day from a too-high school bench, especially when the school day began at eight in the morning and lasted till five in the afternoon.

39

French fathers boasted that they sent their boys to school to learn to think for themselves, not to think other people's thoughts, but to solve their own problems. Louis and Jean did some thinking. They solved the problem of the too-high benches. They found that if they sat on one foot during history period, and on the other during arithmetic, and swung both feet to the rhythm of the songs during music session, they got along very well.

Since Monsieur Becheret, the teacher, lectured one day and questioned the next, Louis did not find it too difficult to compete with his sighted classmates. After a few weeks he stood at the top of most of his classes.

In arithmetic he could often work a problem in his head as quickly as the other pupils on paper. But when it came to the reading and writing periods there was nothing for him to do. There were no books for blind boys to read and no way for them to write. This he learned the first day of school. When the primers were passed out, he held out his hand and was given one. He touched Jean to see how the reading was done. He held his book the same way, but the pages told him no magic words.

"Are there no books for blind boys to read?" he asked the teacher.

40

When Monsieur Becheret said, "None that I know of," Louis put his head down on his desk and wept. "Don't feel bad," comforted his classmates, "we'll read your lessons to you."

After school the boys and girls hurried home to *goûter*, an afternoon snack, usually a slice of bread and butter, but sometimes a crusty roll and piece of chocolate. Then they did homework until suppertime and afterward till bedtime. Louis's school friends took turns with Marie being eyes for him during the evening study periods.

Monsieur Becheret was not only schoolteacher for the village, he also acted as bellringer, distributed holy water to the homes, and wound the ancient town clock. Sometimes he took Louis with him on his round of duties. Louis liked the feel of the big brass key that wound the clock. He enjoyed the friendly visits as they distributed holy water. Occasionally, a good housewife gave him a sweet roll. But best of all he liked to hold the rope when Monsieur Becheret rang the bells, the solemn call of the Angelus three times a day, and once in a while, pleasure of pleasures, a lusty carillon of all the bells announcing a wedding.

Louis was sorry when his school days under Monsieur Becheret in the village school were over. Jean and the other ten-year-old boys could go on to academic schools, but those schools were not for boys without sight.

One day the Abbé Palluy called at the farmhouse with an exciting suggestion. Louis was sitting in the fireplace corner weaving a multicolored fringe for a new harness. The abbé examined his careful work and then turned to his parents:

"Would you like your son to have advanced education? To be taught music and a trade?" He told them of a school in Paris of which he had recently heard, a school where blind youths could obtain advanced education and learn useful trades.

"We would be pleased to have our son attend a school of advanced education," said Simon René.

"Oh yes, very pleased," said Monique.

Louis could keep still no longer. He *had* to know. "Will there be books at the school I can read for myself?"

"I have heard," said the abbé, "that a group of blind students from the school once read from books before the king and queen, and played music on various instruments."

The weaving frame clattered to the floor. Louis jumped up knocking his stool over. "When may I go, Papa? May I go soon?"

A letter was sent to the Royal Institution for Blind Youth in Paris requesting admission. Several days later word was received from Dr. Sebastian Guillé, director of the school, stating Louis had been granted a scholarship, and the date set for his entrance was February 15, 1819.

It was Louis's first ride in a stagecoach. Often he had been at the village square when the coach came in but never had he been a passenger. He enjoyed it all, from the sharp commands of the driver out front, as he guided his four-horse team, to the jounce and sway of the lumbering vehicle itself. The clop-t-clop of the horses' hoofs on the hard ground beat out a rhythm to the words that kept singing in his thoughts. "Books to read! Books to read!"

His father described the Île de France countryside, white with hoarfrost, as they rode along. He told of hills dotted with poplar groves, of flat lowlands through which flowed the greenish water of the broad river Marne, of stone walls that divided pastures from stubble fields where wheat and oats and rye had grown during the summer.

The stagecoach stopped for passengers at Lagny. Louis whispered, "Abbé Palluy told me there is a famous old church here."

"It dates back to the thirteenth century," said Simon René, "and has many old inscriptions."

After four hours of travel from Coupvray, the stage-coach pulled up at the Gate of the Trone, Paris. Simon René and Louis got out and inquired the way to the school on Saint-Victor Street. The smoke-heavy air and the noisy hurry of the city were very strange after the clear atmosphere and country quiet of Coupvray.

At last they stood before a narrow four-story, gray, stone building. They rapped the door-knocker and entered. Louis felt the cold dampness of the stone walls and held his father's hand a little tighter.

The caretaker led them up the stone steps to the director's office.

"Come in, my friends," invited Dr. Guillé. "We have been expecting you." As they sat together, the director explained the routine of the school. Then he took them through the boys' section of the building, the better classrooms, the chapel, and the dining room. Some doors Dr. Guillé did not open.

Simon René took note of the dark, overcrowded condition of the school, but since there was no other of its kind in France, and since the director and the teachers appeared to be devoted to their work, he decided to enroll his son. After an affectionate embrace he set out for home alone.

As Louis listened to his retreating footsteps, panic seized him. He wanted to run after those friendly footfalls, but the director was speaking to him. . . .

"Come, Louis, you and I shall go to the geography class."

Dr. Dafau, the assistant director, was telling the class such interesting things about France, Louis forgot he was far from home among people he didn't know. The fear that had been pressing in on him gradually went away. But that night as he lay in his assigned place in the long row of iron cots, homesickness smothered him like thick gray fog. He longed for his parents, his bed in the garret, the bongs of the friendly village clock. Tears came in spite of his effort to keep them back.

A boy nearby heard and tiptoed over to sit with him. "I felt like you when I first came last year," he whispered. "But you'll learn to like it here. It's a good school. We'll be friends. My name is Gabriel Gauthier."

Louis no longer felt alone. He had a friend. He went to sleep.

The next morning he was thrilled to find that his first class was to be a reading class. At last he would learn to read books for himself! A servant brought in a huge book weighing many pounds and placed it on a reading stand. The pages were embossed with large capital letters which the pupils read by passing their fingers over them to seek out their shape and then spell them into words. It was a slow process, but nevertheless it was reading.

Louis learned quickly. In a short time he had read the few books assigned to his class. He went to the director. "Please, Dr. Guillé, may I have more books to read?"

"There are no more books for you, my boy. The raised-letter books, they take up so much room and are so expensive to make, it isn't possible to have many."

"But *Docteur*, isn't there some way to make books so that blind boys can have as many books to read as other boys?"

"No one has yet found a way," said the director, "but that is a problem for grown-ups." He seemed annoyed. "There are other things for you to do besides read books. You shall learn to knit, and make slippers, and play the piano."

Louis's nimble fingers soon mastered the knitting and slipper-making. Each day he waited eagerly for the time assigned him on the piano. But he must learn by ear or by having a teacher guide his hands; there was no music blind boys could read.

"If only I could write out my music and store it on

47

a shelf instead of having to keep it all in my head," he complained to Gabriel.

"And these long arithmetic problems! If only I could figure them on paper; they make my head ache," said Gabriel.

"There must be some way, if only we could discover it," said Louis, "for us blind boys to write music, and figures, and even books."

School days were filled to the minute with classes, shop, and music, except for one hour's play period in the afternoon. Louis gaily took part in the games. He was lithe at *saute-mouton* (leap-sheep) and *courses en sac* (sack races). He enjoyed matching wits in a close checker or chess game. The checkers and chess men were identified by pins and notches instead of color. A jolly round dance was always a favorite; it reminded him of Market Day at home.

Thursday afternoons were field day. The students lined up along a rope. They dubbed themselves the "rope gang." An instructor walked at the head of the procession as it made its way, like a huge centipede, to the city botanical gardens. There they enlarged their knowledge of the outside—new sounds, new smells, new shapes.

Trees were identified by texture of bark and outline

48

of leaf; daisies, hollyhocks, and lilacs by their perfume. It was always a challenge to see who could find the first violet when the walks took them to wooded areas.

The boys always saved a part of their luncheon bread to share with the many pigeons which strutted on the grass. Pigeons were fun, with their whirring of wings, their constant talk-talk, the peck of blunt beaks as the more daring took proffered crumbs from outstretched hands.

Keen ears soon learned to identify many birds by their calls: the mournful note of the turtledove, the loud clear cry of the whippoorwill, the two notes of the chiffchaff. But the bird sound Louis would always like best was the swallow's shrill call.

School closed in July. Louis had not only learned to *like* the school as Gabriel predicted he would, he *loved* it. He loved it in spite of its smelly dampness, in spite of the strict program. He had found that there was no coaxing or pampering under Director Guillé's watchful eye. When the awards were given out, he received certificates for knitting and slipper-making. Gabriel had earned a prize in piano playing. The boys promised to get their sighted brothers and sisters to write letters for them during vacation. "If only we had some way of doing our own writing." Louis sighed. "We could write oftener."

Two months of vacation! Two whole months to breathe Coupvray's clean air and soak up its sunshine! Louis greeted his mother with a kiss on each cheek. He promised his father reams of fringe and bundles of tassels. He visited Jean and the neighbors and the Abbé Palluy.

There was one empty spot in his homecoming. Marie Céline had married and moved to a home of her own. However, on Sundays, not only Marie, but Catherine and Simon and their families came home, and they all went to church together. It was good to hear the Abbé Palluy's voice conducting the service, and to meet Monsieur Becheret and the marquis at the door. They shook hands with him and inquired about his school.

The days and weeks of summer sped by. Once again Louis boarded the weekly stagecoach for Paris, but this time he wasn't venturing into the unknown. He was returning to friends and his second home.

CHAPTER

6

Louis Makes a Resolution

Louis sat up in bed. He couldn't think for a minute where he was. Was he in the upstairs room of the farmhouse or . . . and then he remembered. This was the first day of his third term of school. It had now been almost two years since he enrolled at the Institution for Blind Youth. This year he would be an advanced student.

He turned an inquisitive ear toward the cot next to him. A stirring and a muffled yawn came from it. Good! Gabriel, too, was awake.

Both boys hurriedly put on their new school uniforms, trousers and coats of black cloth, each year a size larger than the one before. They stopped in the washroom long enough to splash their faces with cold water and run combs through unruly hair. Louis's was blond and curly, Gabriel's black and straight. Then the usual *petit déjeuner* (little breakfast) of hot milk and a roll, and they were off to register.

Besides the regular courses in mathematics, grammar, history and Latin, Louis enrolled in cello and organ. He was again assigned work in the slipper factory. He would also learn to braid the long blacksnake whips used in driving oxen. The slippers and whips and other articles made by the students were sold to help meet school expenses.

Now that he was lined up in studies and work, he could ask the question he had been eager to ask all morning. "What books," he inquired, "will there be for me to read this year?"

"Always it's the books, books, books, you are interested in," said his counselor. "You should meet Valentin Haüy, the man who embossed the first books and founded this school."

"Oh, do you know him, Monsieur?" To meet Valentin Haüy, the originator of books for the blind, was his greatest wish.

"I trained under him," said the counselor, "before he went to Germany and Russia to help organize schools such as this in those countries."

"Is he quite old?" Louis asked hoping to prolong the

conversation and find out all he could about the great teacher.

"Yes, he is very old now and feeble, almost blind. He has returned to France to spend his last days." The counselor paused and then suggested, "Have you heard the story of the morning when Valentin Haüy decided to spend his life helping blind folk get an education?"

"No, Monsieur, but I would like very much to hear it. Very much."

The counselor got up, closed the door of his room, and pulled up a chair for Louis.

"It all began on a September morning when Valentin Haüy, then a young man, went for a walk to enjoy the crisp fall air. On his walk he saw a crowd gathered in front of a café in the market of Saint-Ovide. He stopped to see what amused them so. What he saw made him angry."

"What did he see?" asked Louis.

"On a raised platform, ten weary blind men were making sport of their handicap to entertain the onlookers and draw patrons for Saint-Ovide. Someone had dressed them in flowing robes to represent scholars, then put cardboard-rimmed spectacles with no glass on their noses, dunce caps on their heads, and, as a last insult, attached asses' ears to their heads.

"The blind men pretended to read the words and music of a song placed upside down on a stand in front of them. They sang in an out-of-tune chant as they sawed away on the raspy strings of a violin and cello."

"Why would blind men do such a thing?" interrupted Louis.

"Blind men in those days had only about two choices to earn a living, to act as mummers or beg. By their performance on the platform in front of the café, the ten blind men made a living for the man that led them about and eked out an existence for themselves."

Louis leaned forward in his chair. "What—what did Valentin Haüy say to the men?"

"He said, 'I will substitute the truth for the fable. I will make the blind to read ... they shall give harmonious concerts. You men, who put asses' ears on the unfortunate to degrade their heads, I will attach them to yours.' "

Louis laughed. "*Le brave homme! Le brave homme!* (The good man! The good man!)," he shouted. "Then did he start the school?"

"It was then that he made up his mind, but first it was necessary for him to learn how to teach those who do not see with their eyes, how to make books that could be read by touch, and finally how to support a school.

He visited the homes of the wealthy blind and learned all he could. Then he gathered a group of blind children and began the school, this very school that you now attend. The children learned to read the embossed books, to make useful articles, and to sing. They gave concerts before nobility who in turn supported the school."

"The Abbé Palluy told us about the concerts; he said the children once read and sang before the king and queen."

"That is true, but when the revolution came there was no nobility or king and queen to sing for. It was necessary to teach the children some of the songs of the revolution that they might sing on the streets. To keep the school going during those troublous times, Valentin Haüy gave all that he had, and ate but one meal a day."

Louis longed to meet such a man. He hopefully suggested, "Perhaps he will visit our school?"

"I wish it might be so, but the doors have been closed against him."

Louis clenched his fists. "Why—why would the doors be closed against him?"

"Because of those songs he taught during the revolution. Now that there is again a king on the throne, the director says it might be displeasing to him for Valentin

Haüy to visit the school." The counselor sighed. "We who worked with him go to see him and comfort him. He is heartbroken because he is not allowed to visit his first school."

Louis hoped that he would be asked to go along on one of the visits but the counselor said no more. He became busy with papers on his desk, and Louis went to find Gabriel and tell him what he had learned.

During the weeks that followed, as Louis read and re-read the three or four books assigned to that year's work, he often thought of the story the counselor had told him about Valentin Haüy. He wished something would happen to make it possible for him to talk to the originator of embossed books. In an unexpected way he was to have his wish.

Dr. Guillé was dismissed as director of the Royal Institution for Blind Youth. There were rumors that he had mixed his private affairs too much with those of the school.

The students were not sorry to see him go. They would remember him as a stern man who often put them on rations of dry bread and water, or had them thrashed for even trivial school pranks. Louis, being naturally full of fun, had had his share. But above all, they would remember that it was Dr. Guillé who had shut the school doors against Valentin Haüy. They felt the songs of the revolution were only an excuse to keep the old man away.

Dr. Pignier was chosen to be director. Louis went to the first assembly with troubled questioning. What would this new director be like? Would the program of the school be disrupted? Would he insist on substituting his ways for those they were accustomed to?

Louis listened intently as Dr. Pignier gave his opening address. After but a few sentences he felt reassured. He told himself that such a friendly quiet voice, such humble sincere words, could come only from a kind and generous heart. Here was a man the school would learn to love and respect. When, a few assemblies later, Dr. Pignier suggested that the school plan a day-long celebration to pay homage and honor to the school's founder, Valentin Haüy, Louis knew he had been right about the new director.

August twenty-first (1821) was the date agreed upon. With growing excitement the faculty and students, together with Dr. Pignier and the assistant director, Dr. Dafau, worked on the program. It was good they had several months in which to plan and rehearse. Each part of the program would recall some cherished memory of their guest of honor. The leading feature would be a cantata which Valentin Haüy and his pupils had given on Saint Valentine's Day the very first year of the school. After the program, everyone would have a chance to meet the man who was already known on the continent as "the Father of the Blind."

Louis was thrilled. Every day he thought of what he would say when he met the man of books. He practiced hard on his cello. No false note of his should mar the program. His father and Simon would be there to hear him perform. Afterward he would go home with them for the remainder of the summer.

August twenty-first dawned with a cloudless sky, promising a hot day. Early in the morning a platform and benches were set up out of doors in the shade. Soon parents began to arrive. Louis saw to it that his father and Simon sat near his end of the platform. When everything was ready, and the students in their places, Dr. Pignier ushered in and seated the guest of honor.

As the opening chords of the cantata poured forth in perfect unison from full orchestra and chorus, Valentin Haüy was almost overcome with joyful recognition. It was as if the hero of long wars had come home to be crowned at last in a burst of glory.

No one thought of the heat, as solos, recitatives, interludes, and choruses followed each other. Every student in the school had a part, either in chorus or orchestra or both. Louis wiped the perspiration from his forehead but was aware only of his cello as its voice blended into the harmonious whole. The cantata was near perfect, and of course given from memory. The long months of practice paid off.

The conclusion of the program was a tribute in verse to the school's founder. Valentin Haüy was too overcome to make a speech in reply. All he could say was, "Give not the honor to me, my children; it is God who has done all."

Simon René gave Louis the only praise he wanted to hear. "Well done, my son, well done. I wish your mother could have heard you."

Simon went with Louis to put the cello away. "I'm proud of you, my brother," he said.

Then came the part of the day Louis had been looking forward to, the time when the students could meet and talk to Valentin Haüy. One by one they passed by. Valentin Haüy took time to visit with each asking his name and what he studied. Louis, who had wanted to say so much to this man, when his turn came, could think of nothing to say. He stood with his hand clasped in the old teacher's and barely answered his questions.

59

The spell of the day was still on him as he rode in the stagecoach between his father and Simon. He was unusually quiet, lost in thoughts of his own. He couldn't forget the clasp of the master's hand. Somehow he felt the handshaking had been like the game of "Button,

button, who has the button?"—the button representing Valentin Haüy's work. It seemed to him the great teacher had left the button in his hand. Yes, in *his* hand, and he only twelve!

That night in the swaying old stagecoach Louis made a resolution. He resolved he would find a way—as Valentin Haüy had made it possible for blind students to read a *few* books—he would find a way for them to read *many* books.

"Sleepy, Louis?" asked Simon René, evidently thinking that to be the reason his usually gay and talkative son was so quiet.

"Yes, Papa," said Louis, wishing to be alone with the tremendous new thoughts he was thinking.

From that night on, Louis spent every spare minute both at home and at school trying to devise an alphabet code, a way of writing, that would make possible many books, great libraries of books for those who must read with their fingers.

CHAPTER 7

"Must Someone Always Read to Me?"

TWO YEARS had gone by since the program for Valentin Haüy. The great master was dead. Louis was again on his way home for summer vacation. He was now fourteen but as yet had found no solution to the resolution he had made as he rode home in the stagecoach the night after the program. He had devised no alphabet code or way of writing that would make possible *many* books for finger readers. He welcomed vacation time, there would be more hours for experimenting.

The stagecoach was early, and his father was not at the village square to meet him. But no matter, he was on familiar ground. He hurried down steep Touarte Street.

As he opened the low oak door of the farmhouse,

he was welcomed by the savory smells of his favorite foods. He knew they had been cooked especially for him. His mother met him at the door.

"I say, Mama, no kitchen ever smelled half so good as yours," and he gave the pleased cook a sound kiss on each cheek.

"How you have grown, Louis! I scarcely come above your shoulder."

"Aha, and that might not be saying much for my height. All told, you are scarcely more than an armful." He proved it to the delighted but flustered little woman.

"Your mother may be petite," said Simon René, who had just come in from the harness shop, "but she is as strong as a little thoroughbred horse."

"And as pretty," added Louis who had his own ideas of beauty.

"It's good to have you home again, son," said Simon René giving Louis an extra hug. "The old house has a lonesomeness these days with all the children gone. Is it not so, Mama?"

"Oh yes," Monique agreed, "a great lonesomeness. Now sit to the table, both of you, and eat before the soup gets cold. We shall not be lonesome tonight."

Louis and his parents sat long at the table and talked; and then again under the tree by the kitchen door, they

63

visited late into the night. His father and mother were eager to hear the details of the school year and the progress Louis had made. Of course there had been letters from him, but those letters had been written through another, a sighted person, and therefore with reserve. Now they could have the whole truth.

And Louis in turn felt he could, without seeming conceited, tell them, his own parents, about the honors he had received—the prizes in music, the promotions in studies, the new position of foreman in the slipper factory. It had been a good year and he told all.

"And now, Papa, what about the harness shop? What is on the workbench for tomorrow?"

"Tomorrow there will be nothing. The day is yours. One thing you will want to do is visit the Abbé Palluy. Only yesterday he was asking when you would be home. We owe him much."

Mid-morning of the next day found Louis making his way up the narrow cobblestone street. He walked confidently with his head up, breathing deeply of the clean country air, while his cane sought out the familiar landmarks—doorsteps of neighbors, the market place, the water trough, the church. Unerringly he turned in at the old presbytery where he had been a daily visitor when a small boy, and rapped the door-knocker.

The abbé himself answered the door.

"Come in, come in, my son. There is no one I would rather see this fine morning. How goes the school?

And that friend of yours, Gabriel Gauthier? The slipper factory? And the music? Let us sit in my study while you give an account of yourself."

Louis laughed. "Answering in the order you ask, Father, the old school grows older; the halls remain chilly and damp; the little roaches run at night. We're lucky if it isn't rats. There are so many students, if the walls were not made of stone they would bulge like a barrel. Water is still scarce. We are allowed only one bath a month. But in spite of the inconveniences we like it. Gabriel is fine and sends his greetings. He advances fast in music. As to the slipper factory, you are now speaking to the new foreman."

"Congratulations, my son, I believe the work in your father's harness shop prepared you for that. Now let's hear about the music."

"Music? Everyone at school has a chance but I fear you might not always call it music. You would put your fingers in your ears during practice hours. There are several pianos going in the big room at the same time, while one boy plays the bassoon on the stair-landing, another a flute in the window recess, and I add my cello notes from the farthest corner I can find. But the organ is my favorite. In the chapel and alone, it lets my heart speak."

"*Tiens*, we shall go over to the church presently and you shall play for me. Are there any problems other than the outgrown building?"

"No new problems." Louis sighed. "Just the same old one, but it grows larger and larger. We blind boys can never hope to have an education equal to sighted boys unless we can have books—music books, history books, books of all kinds—whole libraries of books."

"There are some books at the school, are there not?"

"Fourteen, to be exact, plus a few arithmetics. Valentin Haüy made the original plates. They are huge volumes embossed in the large letters of the sighted. The fingers must trace the letters and the reader spell the words as he moves slowly across the page. Many volumes are required to transcribe a small ink print book. They are too expensive to make, and take up too much room ever to have many. Besides," and Louis chuckled, "a boy would be an old man before he got through a twelve-volume set of history at the rate he could read embossed-letter books."

"Do you have an idea as to how more books might be possible?"

"Only if someone can discover a simpler alphabet than the embossed letters. Letters that can be read by fingertips as quickly as the eye of the seeing reads print."

"You have worked on such an alphabet, have you not?"

"Oh yes, always in my spare time I try to figure out an alphabet code, but I have gotten nowhere, nowhere at all."

They sat in silence. Presently, Louis stood up and ran his hands longingly over the ponderous volumes lining the abbé's study. "Will I never, never, be able to read books like these for myself? Must someone always read to me?"

"Only God knows the answer, my son. Trust Him. I feel confident He has something very special in store for you."

So saying the abbé also stood up; he and Louis walked over to the church to play the organ.

All summer long, when Louis was not busy making fringes and tassels for the harnesses, he worked on an alphabet code. He cut circles, triangles, and squares from leather. He tried small nail heads. He experimented with the signs of the zodiac for music. But nothing was quite right.

Depressed by weeks of frustrated effort, he returned to school in October with the problem still unsolved. He had almost decided the "something special" God had in mind for him was *not* devising an alphabet for finger readers.

CHAPTER

8

Six Embossed Dots

LOUIS AND GABRIEL TOOK their places in the classroom along with the fifty-eight other students Dr. Pignier had called together for an "important assembly."

What did the director want of them? No one seemed to have the least hint of what to expect: a reprimand, new regulations, or perchance a prominent visitor was coming to the school? As they waited, their curiosity grew.

At the sound of a familiar footfall coming down the hall all whispering stopped. Each face turned toward the front of the room.

"I have here," said the quiet voice of the director, "some samples of a special kind of writing that Captain Charles Barbier of the army left with me to show you.

He first used the writing to transmit orders to his soldiers during night maneuvers. It is a code of dots and dashes that can be read in the dark by touch so that his soldiers need not betray their position to the enemy by making a light. Captain Barbier thought you might find his system usable. He calls it Sonography since it is based on sounds."

Dr. Pignier passed out the sample pages on which the writing appeared as hump-like dots and dashes. The dots and dashes had been pressed into heavy paper by means of an instrument something like a blunt darning needle, called a stylus.

When Louis felt the embossed dots beneath his fingers, he wanted to shout and dance! He clutched Gabriel's arm. "This is it! This is it!" he whispered.

This was what he had been searching for. Embossed *dots* were the answer to reading and writing for finger readers. But not the captain's Sonography system. It was based on phonics, a certain number of dots to each sound in a word. But there were too many dots to the unit, as many as twelve, making the reading difficult and slow, and taking up too much space ever to have many books. No one would learn to spell. And there was no provision for numbers, accents, or music notation. It did have the advantage over the Valentin Haüy embossed letter system in that it could be written, but the writing was very slow because of the many dots to punch, and the dashes were hard to make.

Dots—dots—dots! Louis thought, wrote, and dreamed dots! At night when the even breathing of the other boys indicated they were asleep, and the monitor had made his last round, Louis retrieved his writing board and stylus from under the mattress where he had hidden them, and experimented on an alphabet code, using the magic dots. Each letter must be represented by a group of dots *few* enough to be entirely under the fingertip. Then the blind reader's finger could glide across the page taking in a line at a time as does the sighted reader's eye.

Often the rumble of the milkman's wagon on the cobbles would announce to Louis that it was dawn and that he had worked all night. He quickly slipped the board back in hiding and tried to get a few minutes' sleep.

When vacation time came, he went home thin and pale from the sleepless nights. He had a bad cough. Monique was worried. She insisted on full nights of rest, and proved a more watchful monitor than the one at school. Sleep in Coupvray's fresh air, and walks in the country, together with his mother's good cooking, soon had him feeling better.

Every free hour he worked on the new alphabet. Sometimes he sat on the hillside above the village, but his favorite spot was the stone step of the harness shop. With the rhythmic sound of his father's mallet he felt a companionship in work. There, too, he could hear

his mother singing old French ballads as she churned, wove cloth, or did other tasks in the house. The songs were soothing and reassuring, especially on those days when he had to back up and begin over again. The village clock kept him informed of his progress in hours.

He often wished he could discuss his work with the Abbé Palluy but that dear friend had passed away. The neighbors thought his dot-punching some sort of solitaire he had invented to while away the hours.

François' ox wagon with its solid wooden wheels creaked by. *"Bonjour,* Louis, still making the pinpricks, I see."

"That I am, François, but they are most finished, I think." Louis's nose told him the farmer was taking apples to market. Apples reminded him of October, and October meant he would soon be going back to school. He worked a little faster.

That evening he carefully reviewed his work on the alphabet, step by step. As a basis he had used a code key of six embossed dots, $\begin{smallmatrix} 1 & 4 \\ 2 & 5 \\ 3 & 6 \end{smallmatrix}$ three high and two wide. He tested the key again to make sure his fingertip could easily span it without any up or down exploring.

The first ten letters had been the most difficult. He had made them from different arrangements of the top

73

four dots of the key. A was dot one, B dots one and two, C dots one and four. . . .

A	B	C	D	E	F	G	H	I	J

The next ten letters were easy to make but a little more difficult to read. He had simply added dot three of the key to each of the first ten letters:

K	L	M	N	O	P	Q	R	S	T

The last five were made by adding dots three and six to the first five letters, A—E:

U	V	X	Y	Z

The letter W was omitted since it was seldom used in French. Later when an Englishman requested him to make up a sign for W, he chose letter R written backwards: W

The French accented letters were the next problem; each must be given a symbol in dots.

He worked on a number sign and decided on a combination of dots 3, 4, 5, and 6: By placing the number sign before each of the first ten letters they became numbers. He was experimenting on music notation when it was time to go back to school.

Hurriedly he made copies of the alphabet to take to the boys. What would they say? The letters were so simple, he wondered why it had taken so long to figure them out. He breathed a sigh of relief. His resolution made three years before in the stagecoach had been kept. He had devised an alphabet that gave promise of *many* books.

With a sharp awl Louis had blinded himself and created his problem of reading and writing; with a dull awl he had solved it. *He was fifteen!*

Back at school Gabriel was the first to learn of the new alphabet.

"Louis, *c'est merveilleux! C'est magnifique!* (It is marvelous! It is magnificent!) And it is so simple I can learn it in but a half hour. You will truly receive the Legion of Honor for this!"

Gabriel called the other boys to come and *see*. Soon a group was gathered around Louis. They were all enthusiastic and eager to learn the new alphabet. They began telling what it would do for them.

"We can take notes in class," said one.

75

"We can write our own compositions," said another, "and better still, read what we have written. We can take dictation and—"

"I'll keep my own diary," interrupted an older boy. "No more will Mademoiselle Nosey pry into my private life. Always it's 'Have you nothing to say about Yvonne, today?'"

The boys laughed. "And then does she tell Yvonne?"

"I don't know but from now on I'll write my own secrets, and only I shall read them. What freedom!"

76

He stretched his arms wide as if trying to measure this new-found independence.

"My sighted sister will learn the new writing," said a boy from Normandy, "and then I can read my own letters from home."

"True, true," agreed the boys.

"We can keep our own accounts and work page-long arithmetic and algebra problems," suggested another who liked mathematics.

Gabriel had been quiet for some time but now he demanded attention. "Already I know the alphabet. I have written a sentence":

The boys began comparing their copies of the alphabet with what Gabriel had written. He was almost mobbed with everyone wanting to try to read it. Finally one of the boys shouted, "I know what you wrote. It says, 'I can write.' "

"*Bien! Bien!* (Fine! Fine!) Before tomorrow we'll all be able to write."

Dr. Pignier sent for Louis.

"What is this new system of writing I hear you have invented? Aren't you going to show it to me?"

"Oh yes, *Docteur*, I will be pleased to show you if you will dictate something for me to write."

"Suppose you try this paragraph from the *Moniteur*."

Louis punched the paragraph into dotted code as Dr. Pignier read at medium speed. He then turned the paper over and, gliding his fingers over the embossed dots, read it back to the director.

"It is remarkable, my boy, truly remarkable! Keep on with your research. I will do all I can to help you."

Dr. Pignier had slates made to fit the writing. Letters could be punched in the windows of the slate keeping them uniform in size and in a straight line. He applied to the Ministry of the Interior requesting that Louis Braille's alphabet be made the official method of reading and writing in the school.

Goverment bureaus are often slow to change established customs. Year after year Dr. Pignier renewed his request, with no result. The school, however, used the fast new system of writing almost exclusively in its daily program. But since Valentin Haüy's embossed letter system was official, a knowledge of it also had to be taught.

Louis felt anxious about the delay. Surely the bureau would adopt the new system of dot writing. But could he be sure?

CHAPTER

9

The Professor

LOUIS STOOD IN THE DOORWAY of the slipper shop. A ray of sunshine, filtered by the city's haze, stole between the roofs of tall buildings and found his face. Its warmth relaxed him and made him lose himself in thoughts far removed from the work at hand. He was not aware of the young learner's question about the slipper until the boy touched him.

"I'm sorry, Edouard, what was it you asked? I must have been daydreaming."

Time and again during the last few weeks this had happened. He must shake himself out of it and be alert when at work. The thinking would have to wait for free time; but there was so much crowding his mind these days.

He was almost twenty, a dividing point between youth and manhood, an age when he should be deciding on his future. What did it hold for him? He wished for a definite work of his own, a definite income. It irked him to continue being dependent on his father or the school.

True, he had helped pay his way. At home he worked in the harness shop; at school he had been foreman of the slipper factory since he was fourteen, and had done student teaching. But this was all in the nature of being a helper. He wanted his *own* ship of work to captain and guide. In what direction should he seek it—music, teaching, or shop work? Openings for a young blind man were almost non-existent, and so the periods of long, long thoughts.

One day Dr. Pignier called him to his office. As Louis seated himself in the same chair where he had demonstrated his alphabet five years before, he had the fleeting thought that this was his good-luck chair.

"I am pleased to inform you," said the director, "that at the last meeting with the Minister of the Interior you were chosen to become apprentice teacher. The salary will be small at first, fifteen francs per month, but both your position and salary should grow. In time you will become a regular teacher, a professor on full salary."

Dr. Pignier shook his hand. "Success to you, my son. I have every confidence in you."

Louis was jubilant. His ship was launched—a professor-ship. He would put all he had into it.

When Louis told his family the good news, Simon René threw his arms around him in a joyous embrace. "Mama, did you hear that? Did you hear, Mama? Our little boy will be a professor after all. A professor! A professor! Like the wine grower said the day he was registered. Who would have believed it?"

Monique wiped her eyes with her checkered apron. "Thank the good God! Thank the good God!"

October found Louis as teacher in the classroom with every seat filled and more children trying to crowd in. "We want to be in his class," they told Dr. Pignier. "He is blind like us. He knows how to explain things so that we understand."

Louis taught classes in grammar, geography, arithmetic, and his embossed dot writing, also piano and cello. Next to his system of dot writing, without which it would have been almost impossible for him to teach, he found his fund of stories his greatest help. He sent word to Catherine: "Your stories, Big Sister, and those of the Abbé Palluy are worth more than a chest of rare treasure."

A dull class in arithmetic could be sharpened to the
working point by a witty story. "Nothing like a good
laugh to clear the mind," Louis always said. History
came alive under the story brush. A boy caught in
dishonesty was more apt to right-about-face after hear-
ing one of the abbé's stories of honesty than receiving
the usual caning. A tale told at the bedside of a sick
boy in the morning gave him something to think about
during the day, and a promise of one in the evening,
something to look forward to.

Hippolyte Coltat, one of the older students, became a best friend. He and Gabriel often came to Louis's room of an evening to have some music and air their views on the happenings of the day. But the evening invariably ended the same: "Now, Louis, one of your tales and we'll take ourselves off to bed."

Every week Louis enjoyed his teaching more and more, especially so after Gabriel and Hippolyte were taken on as apprentice teachers with him. Their lives were not too different from that of the students. They were under many of the same regulations: their mail was censored, they must be in at a certain hour, they ate with the students, and wore the same basic uniform of black cloth, with the addition of silk and gold braid. They did, however, have rooms to themselves.

The three apprentice teachers were aware that their teaching was an experiment. If they made good, the position of teacher would be open to other blind young people. They worked accordingly. Dr. Pignier wrote of their excellent progress to the Department of the Interior. He counseled and guided them, invited them often to his home, and took them out to entertainments that they might become adjusted to the social world of the sighted.

The weeks and months, a year, went by.

It was during the afternoon of the thirty-first of May, Louis's second year of teaching, that there came a knock on his classroom door.

"I will take over your class," said Dr. Pignier. "Your brother waits to speak with you in my office."

Louis was immediately apprehensive. Why would Simon come without writing first? Something must be wrong at home.

The brothers embraced. Then Simon made known his errand. "Our father," he said, "passed away this morning." Moments of tense silence elapsed. . . . "His last words, Louis, were of you."

When Dr. Pignier rejoined them, Simon handed him a message the dying father had dictated. It was a letter commending his blind son to the director's care. "Please never forsake him," the letter implored. As he listened, Louis felt the words were written in blood.

Dr. Pignier put his arm around his young teacher's shoulders. "I have long considered Louis a son."

The brothers left for home on the six o'clock stage-coach. They rode in silence, unmindful of the country-side's early spring fragrance or the birds' evening songs. Night was falling when they reached Coupvray. Louis took Simon's arm as they made their way down steep Touarte Street to the lower village.

The low oak door of the farmhouse opened to the sound of weeping and the smell of burning candles. Louis clasped his sorrowing mother in his arms, and then went to kneel by the bed in the alcove where lay the best father a boy could ever have.

All the village of Coupvray attended the funeral. They came to pay their respects to the craftsman who had lived among them more than sixty years. The church bell tolled solemnly during the service. Louis silently added his prayer to those that were said audibly. As he turned from the grave-side, he was comforted with the thought that his father had left only good memories behind. The next day he helped Simon place a marker on the grave, and then, reminding his mother he would soon be home for the summer vacation, he returned to the Royal Institution for Blind Youth to complete the school term.

In the spring of 1833, having served four to five years as apprentice teachers, the three blind instructors were formally promoted to the status of professor. How Louis wished he could tell his father and again hear him say, "*A professor! A professor!*" No one could ever put so much meaning in the word as his harness-maker father. His salary was now increased to three hundred francs per year.

The blind teachers worked hard for their school. Gabriel headed the music department. Louis and Hippolyte carried major responsibilities in other departments. Louis taught grammar, history, geography, arithmetic, algebra, geometry, piano, and violoncello. His evenings were filled with writing textbooks and a new edition of *Methods of Writing Words, Music, and Plain Songs by Means of Dots.* He spent hours in research. Pages of difficult music were transcribed by his stylus.

He accepted the post of organist at the church of Saint-Nicholas-des-Champs. Being an organist caused him some concern at first, not because of any difficulty in reading the music, but rather of giving proper reverence in worship. From the days of the Abbé Palluy he had been taught to pay close attention to the service, but now he found himself too occupied with stops, pedals, and keyboard. He solved his problem by becoming so familiar with the music, his mind was free to follow the service, and at the same time support it with an enlarging background on the organ. The position of organist at Saint-Nicholas became one of his greatest pleasures to which he looked forward every week. Yet, after holding it for many years, when one of his students was out of work, he gave up the post without hesitation to the needy young man.

"With him," wrote Coltat in his *Notice Biographique sur L. Braille*, "friendship was a conscientious duty. . . . He cultivated it like a rare orchid."

Sometimes being a true friend brought with it unpleasant duties. If a report came to the three friends that a young teacher was following a method that was not good, or failed to be careful about his personal appearance, or had developed a *blind-ism*, Louis was firm that the young man should be counseled, kindly, but not sparing the truth.

In the stress of school life blind students were apt to develop some form of blind-ism—repeated clacking of the tongue, snapping fingers, tapping a foot, or some rhythmic movement of the body. These habits seemed to relieve tension but made the doer appear odd in sighted company. Lucien, a gifted young organist, looked over his embossed music while riding the bus on the way to the church where he played. As his fingers traced the dotted notes across the page, he swung his head like a clock pendulum, accompanying the movement of his fingers, back and forth, back and forth. Sighted children on the bus watched him and tittered. A boy meaningfully tapped his own head.

When such incidents were reported, the question was always asked, "Who will tell him?" If Hippolyte or Gabriel hesitated, as they usually did, Louis would laugh and say, "Come, I'll sacrifice myself." It happened so often that the saying, "Come, I'll sacrifice myself," became a sort of quip among the friends. Gabriel nicknamed him The Censor.

For recreation the teacher-trio often walked down a favorite lane. If the day was cold they stopped at the chestnut vender's stand on the corner. Pockets filled with hot chestnuts kept hands warm, and the nut meats were moist and sweet. To see them sprinting along no one would know they were blind except for the telltale white canes. Their only complaint was voiced by Hippolyte:

"The days need more hours to get everything done."

Louis's heavy work schedule, together with the damp, overcrowded living conditions at the school, finally overbalanced his energy. He became terribly tired and had frequent dizzy spells. When climbing stairs he had to stop often to rest. He tried to ignore the symptoms as a passing slight indisposition, but one night a hemorrhage revealed he was suffering from the first stages of tuberculosis. A lightened work load and rest periods in sunny Coupvray, where his devoted mother nursed him back to a semblance of health, kept him going.

Louis often played the piano at entertainments. He was equally at ease with a ponderous Beethoven number

88

or a peasant gavotte. These evenings introduced him to Paris society. He seemed to adjust to the sighted world better than the sighted adjusted to him. He accepted needed help graciously, but disliked over-hovering or praise mixed with pity—anything that set him apart as an oddity.

The annoying habit of hostesses and also salesmen of speaking to his guide instead of directly to him was a source of irritation. The hostess would inquire of the guide, "Does Monsieur Braille take sugar in his coffee?" Or the salesman would ask, "Does your friend prefer linen or cotton? How much does he wish to pay?"

The guide tried to educate them by pointedly suggesting, "Ask Monsieur Braille. He knows. I do not."

"Why do they do it?" protested Louis. "Because I do not have eyes to see, do they assume I also do not have ears to hear, mouth to answer, or brain to think?"

"I know not," said his guide. "The sighted are truly very stupid at times."

In spite of the satisfaction and joy of teaching there began to grow in Louis's innermost thoughts a sharp, nagging worry. The worry had nothing to do with his health.

Ten years had gone by since the acceptance of the dot alphabet as the reading and writing method of the school,

89

but the Ministry of the Interior had never endorsed it. The embossed-letter system of Valentin Haüy remained the official method of reading. Pupils must still struggle through the slow process of learning to read the old method, a loss of time to them as well as to the teachers.

Louis had been invited to demonstrate his dot-writing at the Exposition of Industry held in Paris, in May, 1834. King Louis-Philippe had visited with him and spoken flattering words for his invention.

Dr. Pignier had written repeatedly to the Ministry of the Interior asking for official recognition of the system. The students had written. Louis had written. The only reply was a pat on the back for the inventor: "This work seems remarkable. Monsieur Braille ought to be encouraged."

Louis's friends shrugged off his uneasiness. "Why do you worry? The dot system is a part of us, a part of the school. No one could separate us from it."

True, *if* Dr. Pignier remained in the director's chair, there was no need for concern. By his sanction the dot alphabet was in use. But Louis was aware of plot and intrigue against the director. He knew that Dr. Pignier's remaining head of the school was doubtful, and that the six-dot system of writing was in danger. He also knew the source of the possible danger.

CHAPTER
10

Louis's Low and High Days

Louis let the last chord of the Couperin prelude die away in the empty chapel and leaned his head against the music ledge of the organ. The minor melody matched his feelings that Wednesday morning, May 20, 1840.

It was the time of year that should have inspired lively tunes—lilting bird songs, bursting buds, and all the things poets write about in May, but neither Louis nor nature was in the mood. Outside, the rain drummed crescendos against the windowpane, while the eaves dripped a monotonous accompaniment on a piece of projecting tin.

"Even the skies are weeping today," he said half-aloud.

What Louis feared would happen, had happened. Dr. Pignier had been dismissed as director of the Institution

91

for Blind Youth. Dr. P. Armand Dafau, the solemn assistant director, had been appointed to fill the vacancy.

Louis knew the gossip behind the scene. Dr. Dafau had become weary of Director Pignier's supposed slowness in getting certain changes put through, of his monk-like strictness in conducting the institution. The past four years Dr. Dafau had been seeking a sufficient excuse to have Dr. Pignier removed and gain the office of director for himself. Recently he and two other members of the staff had settled on a scheme.

A report was drawn up testifying that "Pignier corrupts minds by his history teaching," insinuating the director's instruction was biased since his education had been obtained in the schools of the monks. The Ministry of the Interior had accepted the report and acted accordingly.

Louis loved Dr. Pignier as a second father. The director had cared for him in illness, guided him in his teaching, encouraged and supported him in his research. It was because of Dr. Pignier that the students enjoyed the independence the new alphabet gave them.

Louis had formerly respected Dr. Dafau. It was in his geography class, that first day of school, he had become so interested that he forgot the fear of being left by his father. But somewhere, at some time, he couldn't put his finger on the exact day, he began to suspect that Dr.

Dafau did not approve of the six-dot system of writing. It was nothing he said, but rather that he said nothing.

While others complimented and offered suggestions, the assistant director remained silent. After his suspicion was aroused, Louis took note, and had reached the conclusion that Dr. Dafau was definitely opposed to the new system of reading and writing. What would the director do about it now that he had the authority? Louis wondered, and pondered that May morning as he played the chapel organ and listened to the rain outside.

As the months went by Louis quietly continued his research, and the writing of books in his six-dot system. Director Dafau continued to ignore both. If the new alphabet was called to his attention he dismissed it as of little importance. In his printed report, "The Methods of Reading and Writing Used by the Blind," he made no mention of Louis Braille's method, but rather dwelt on Valentin Haüy's embossed-letter system and Charles Barbier's Sonography.

If, however, Dr. Dafau was the silent enemy of the six-dot alphabet, the students were its applauding friends. They used it daily in all their classwork. They eagerly awaited each new section of the *Précis d'Histoire* and other books that Louis prepared, and made notebooks from them.

The constant strain and depressing uncertainty finally

undermined Louis's already none-too-rugged health. He was forced in the month of April, 1843, to take a six-months' leave of absence. As always, his hard-working, gentle mother was glad for his visit. And as always, he immediately began to feel better under her care and Coupvray's clear country air and sunshine.

He enjoyed especially the Sunday reunions, although the family was now reduced to four of the original six. Marie Céline had died of a fever, leaving two children. Louis visited her grave and his father's in the cemetery adjoining the church, and wondered why some are taken and others left.

He spent many hours in the sun with slate and stylus on the worn stone step of the harness shop where he had worked out his alphabet. Now it was the mallets of Catherine's boys, who had learned their grandfather's trade, that kept him company. Simon preferred farming to harness-making, but if the boys got behind, both he and Louis gave them a hand.

Gauthier and Hippolyte wrote weekly keeping him informed on all the activities of the school. Or did they write *all?* Sometimes Louis wondered. But he refused to give room to troublesome doubts and spent more and more time on the two and a half acres of grapes and land his father had left him. Simon farmed it but Louis trained straggling vines, repaired the stone wall, and kept all accounts.

When Louis returned to Paris in October for the beginning of the fall term of school, he had gained weight, his face was as brown as any farmer's, and he felt like one.

Gabriel and Hippolyte met him at the Gate of the Trone. On the walk to the school they were gay, too gay Louis thought. When they reached his room he said, "Now sit down and tell me what means all this nonsense. You are trying to cover up something. *N'est-ce pas?* (Are you not?)"

When they protested and attempted a change of subject, he interrupted. "You don't fool me, my best friends. You read like books. Something has happened to the alphabet, hasn't it?"

Because they still hesitated he pleaded with them, "Tell me all that your letters didn't. I would rather hear it from you than someone else."

And they told him all, knowing he would have to know sooner or later.

During his absence, Dr. Dafau had brought his hostility against the six-dot system of reading and writing out in the open, the chief grievance against it being that it made the blind independent. He believed if they were independent they would segregate themselves into a world of their own, be their own teachers, run their own schools. . . .

Sighted teachers who were afraid of losing their superior positions, and organists their jobs (Gabriel had already placed more than fifty blind organists in Paris) urged the director to do something about it. Dr. Dafau had complied, and characteristically as in all his reforms, both good and bad, he made a thorough job of it.

All of the school's books had been burned. New ones using embossed letters similar to those of Valentin Haüy's but of a different dimension would replace them. In the future reading would be confined to this medium which sighted teachers could easily follow. No matter that it was a difficult task for the blind, they would have to learn. The six-dot alphabet had been banned except for music. Anyone caught using it would be punished.

The conflict had resolved itself into a contest between the sighted and the blind, with Louis Braille's alphabet the deciding factor. The students refused to give up their alphabet, and of course it couldn't be taken from them and burned as were the books. It was a knowledge they possessed in their minds, and knowledge could not be taken away. Styli could be confiscated but there were plenty of substitutes—darning needles, knitting needles, and nails which could be converted. If punishment were to be meted out, then it would be practically to the whole school. It seemed Dr. Dafau had overstepped himself this time.

Louis was stunned at the recital of events. What a homecoming that October day had proved to be! It was truly his *low* day!

He climbed the worn familiar stairs and automatically carried on his work. Banned were his cherished textbooks. He walked as in a daze. "It can't be so," he told himself. "It must be a dream from which I shall soon awake."

Alone in his room he tried to understand the why of it all, the reasoning of his sighted friends; surely they

97

were friends. He thought of the new school building started under Dr. Pignier and now nearing completion. Was its library of *many* books, for which he had worked, never to be realized? He felt that not only it but the whole future of the blind was being challenged.

And then from somewhere back in his memory beamed a ray of hope, the words of the Abbé Palluy. "Only God knows the answer. Trust Him." Yes, he would trust. He, himself, had been so close to the problem perhaps he could not see it clearly. He would trust the outcome to Him who had the greater perspective. He recalled how the doors of the school had at one time been closed on Valentin Haüy, but eventually everything had worked out. He took courage.

In another part of the building sat a man with graying hair. He was studying the same problem. Dr. Dafau was not so sure now, that he had acted with the best judgment. The assistant director, Dr. Joseph Gaudet, who had joined the staff at the director's request, sat with him. He had made the director see the question from a different viewpoint.

Dr. Gaudet was enthusiastic about the six-dot alphabet. He saw in it a great future for the blind. True, it would make them independent, but should not every citizen of France have the right of equality? Did not the country's motto, "Liberty, Equality, Fraternity," include all of its citizens? Because a man had lost an arm or leg or sight, did that ban him from these privileges? So reasoned Dr. Gaudet with his friend, Dr. Dafau.

A conference was called. The decision favored the blind. The six-dot alphabet was not only freed from its ban but plans were laid to make it the official system of reading and writing in the school. Like a ball, the greater the force with which it is thrown down, the higher it bounces.

The new airy and roomy buildings on 56 Boulevard des Invalides were completed and ready for the Institution of Blind Youth to move in and be at home. The day for the inauguration was set for February 22, 1844. On this day, at the most important program of any building, the recognition of Louis's alphabet was to take place. Dr. Gaudet would officiate, Gabriel Gauthier would have charge of the music.

The auditorium was filled to capacity with students, teachers, relatives, friends, and officials. First came the dedication service, and then Dr. Gaudet arose.

He read a long paper on the systems of reading and writing for the blind, showing the superiority of the six-dot alphabet. A demonstration followed.

Two blind students, a girl and a boy, were sent from the room. A teacher led a little girl, dressed in her black school smock, to the front platform. She was a pretty child with large brown eyes, but the large eyes were of no use to her. They had no sight.

A visitor was invited to dictate an unpublished poem for the little girl to write. Using slate and stylus, she punched the verse into dotted writing on a sheet of firm paper. The girl who had been sent out was called in and handed the poem. She ran her fingers lightly over the embossed dots and read it without hesitation.

Dr. Gaudet next called for a volunteer to dictate a short musical phrase to one of the blind teachers. The auditorium was so still the prick of the stylus could be heard as the melody was punched into the paper. Now the boy was called in and given the embossed music notation. While being guided to the piano, he ran his fingers over the dots. He sat down at the instrument and played the phrase in the proper key and with correct accidentals.

The audience clapped and cheered. They called for the inventor of the marvelous system of writing. When Louis stood up he received a thunderous ovation. It was a wonderful day for him. It was his *high* day.

After the program, Louis respectfully thanked Dr. Gaudet and Dr. Dafau. He shook hands and answered the questions of those who crowded around him. Then he joined the waiting Gabriel and Hippolyte for a celebration of their own.

CHAPTER
11

The Last Years

HAD A MIRACLE HAPPENED? Was he actually freed from the dread tuberculosis? Louis felt it was almost beyond belief.

For a number of years now his health had not permitted him to carry on his teaching. He had been obliged to content himself with music, research, and as he was able, with the transcribing of books for the library.

But in 1847 it seemed a miracle had happened. He was apparently well. The school physician pronounced him able to resume his teaching. Dr. Dafau welcomed him back on the staff. Once again he led classes through the maze of grammar, algebra, history, and music.

From his mother Louis had acquired the habit of careful saving and spending. He managed to put aside from his salary and the income from his land a sum of money which he applied to scholarships for needy students. One such was Pierre.

Pierre showed unusual talent on the organ, and prepared his assignments with exactness. But this day he was having difficulty. Three times he had played F natural for F sharp.

"What goes, Pierre?" asked Louis. "Does your head have a sickness?"

"No, Monsieur, my head has no sickness but my heart has sadness."

Louis laid his hand on the drooping shoulder. "Tell me about it, Pierre."

"The grape harvest, it has failed. There is no longer money. It is necessary that I go home."

"Worry no more," comforted Louis. "I have here a box. It contains a cure for such sickness." He placed the box beside Pierre and told him to open it. Inside were small rolls of paper.

"If you sign a paper like those in the box, your tuition will be paid; the paper says so. It also says if you get work when you finish school, you will repay The Box. How is that for a cure?"

"Oh *merci, merci* (thank you), Monsieur." Pierre eagerly punched his name in dot-writing to the agree-

ment. The paper was rolled and placed in The Box with the other rolls.

"Now do you think you can play the F sharps?"

"Yes, Monsieur, now it will be easy."

Because of the uncertainty of his health Louis put aside any thought of a family and home of his own. He corresponded with his former pupils, told them the news of the school, sent them writing materials and books to copy, paid them from his own funds, and then distributed the books to others. His pupils were his "family," the school was his "home."

Dr. Pignier, in his book, *Notice Biographique sur Trois Professeurs ... de l'Institution des Jeunes Aveugles,* tells of one lady-friend, also blind, in Louis's circle of correspondents. He met her during a trip— perhaps on the stagecoach to Coupvray—and taught her his six-dot system of writing. When they had become good friends, he asked her to be "the dispenser of his charity." In this way those he helped would not know from where the help came. "He never wanted to be thanked."

In 1848, the second revolution broke out in Paris. Suddenly from everywhere muskets were discharged, accompanied with shouts of "To the Republic! To the

Republic!" Barricades were thrown up and the city became a battleground.

Louis and Gabriel followed the events with intense interest. Louis regretted the riots, the hatred, the unnecessary bloodshed, but he felt a republic was the only form of government that would insure equality and liberty for all. He was pleased that the seventy-five-year-old king, Louis Philippe, who had spoken so kindly to him at the Exposition of Industry, when he had demonstrated his alphabet, was able to escape to England. "Gabriel composed a triumphal march," reports one of Louis's biographers, "to the words of Béranger [a well-known French poet] and all France planted trees of liberty singing, 'Queen of the world, O France, O my country.' "

When the turmoil subsided, Louis again returned to research. He was ever conscious of his goal of *many books*. His inventive mind could not rest although medical counsel advised it. Dr. Dafau now did everything he could to help. Different methods of printing the dot writing were being tried out. The Book of Psalms was one of the first books to be printed in dots. Louis had completed a way of writing that could be read by both the sighted and the blind, by outlining the letters used by the sighted according to a standard table of dots, giving the number of dots required to form each letter. He called the system Raphigraphy. It was gladly received by the students who wished to write to sighted friends and relatives. He was now trying to work out a way to trace on paper the clefs and signs of music and write the words of a song parallel to the music. He didn't have time to complete it, and it never has been done. Always he needed more time, more funds.

One day there came through the mail an envelope of official size. Louis felt its wax seal and knew that it would be written in ink; he must find a sighted reader. But to have it read by someone at the school, it may as well be published on a bulletin board. He would get Gabriel and Hippolyte to go with him to Dr. Pignier's home in the late afternoon when the teaching day was over. There he would learn the contents of the letter. Besides, it was high time they were paying a visit to their benefactor.

Dr. Pignier opened the door wide to the trio he had coached as apprentice teachers. He insisted they stay for dinner and afterwards have some music.

Now the seal on the mysterious letter was carefully broken, its contents read. . . . The new Paris-Strasbourg railroad, which had been surveyed two years before, would run through Louis's plot of land in Coupvray. The letter was a statement of compensation for the right of way.

"Wife," called Dr. Pignier toward the kitchen, "break out our best wine. We have need of a toast."

"First an alphabet and now a railroad," said Gabriel. "My friend, what do you bring out of the hat next?"

Louis laughed. "I knew my acres were fertile, but I never expected them to grow a railroad."

If, during the remainder of the evening, Louis had to have a question repeated, his friends understood. Only half of his mind was on the conversation. The other half was busy investing his newly acquired money. He would buy another small piece of land to insure a yearly income, perhaps the plot next to Simon, but there would still be funds for books and research.

Three rewarding years in the classroom went by, and then the miracle of health came to an end. Louis stayed on at the school, teaching a few piano lessons as he was able.

On a December day in 1851, a cold wind brought freezing temperatures to Paris, the same weather as that day almost forty-three years before, when Simon René had made his way up the slippery cobblestone street to register his infant son. Only now there was no sister near to see that he was wrapped "as snug as a moth in a cocoon." Louis caught a severe cold which brought on one hemorrhage after another.

Simon came to be with him in his illness. His mother

was too old to make the trip and Louis was too weak to be moved. Gabriel and Hippolyte were ever close by. Dr. Pignier came often.

As brother and friends sat by his bed, Louis quietly spoke to them:

"Yesterday was one of the most beautiful and greatest of my life. When one has experienced that, he comprehends all the power and majesty of religion. But oh, fathomless mystery of the human heart! I am convinced that my mission is finished on earth; I tasted yesterday the supreme delight; God condescended to brighten my eyes with the splendors of eternal hope. After that, does it not seem that nothing would be able to interest me on earth? *Eh bien!* (Well!) I asked God, it is true, to take me from the world . . . but I felt I was not asking very hard."

The morning of January 6, two days after his forty-third birthday, Louis felt a little stronger. For the past few days, in fact, he had seemed to be improving. He almost dared to hope again.

The joyous clanging of the bells from the spires and belfries of Paris reminded him that it was Epiphany, the day when the visit of the Wise Men from the East to the Babe of Bethlehem is celebrated. He listened to the silvery tones from the tower of the Louvre, the somber strokes from the belfry of Notre Dame, the scale of Saint-Eustache's seven bells, and the triple notes of Saint-Germain des Prés, and all the lesser bells. Louis knew the thrill of the men at the end of the ropes as they sent the clapper symphony into the air. His deep appreciation of the bells dated from his boyhood experience of ringing the Angelus with teacher Becheret.

When the bells were quiet, Louis asked to have repeated to him the symbolic meaning of gold, frankincense, and myrrh, the gifts of the Magi to the infant King on that first Epiphany.

"Gold," said the chaplain, "is the symbol of a gift to a king; frankincense, a gift to a god; and myrrh, a gift for a Man that should die."

Later in the day it appeared that the morning's feeling of strength had been but a foreboding of the end. Louis asked that he might again receive communion.

He knew the time for last good-bys had come. He gave Simon messages of endearment for his mother and sister. To each of those present he whispered words of appreciation and affection. At seven-thirty that evening he died.

Simon left for Coupvray with the sad news. The school prepared for the funeral. The students made a caste of their beloved teacher's face, that they might ever have him with them even though it be but a bronze likeness.

When Simon returned for the funeral, he brought with him his mother's request that Louis be brought home for burial. Once more Louis was to make the journey to Coupvray over the road he had traveled so many times. Once more he was to rest a few hours in the alcove of the stone farmhouse at the foot of steep Touarte Street. After a short service in the church, where he had been baptized and where he had played the organ for the Abbé Palluy, he was buried beside his father and Marie in the humble Coupvray cemetery.

As the sorrowing mother, sister, and brother stood by the grave, the ancient clock, having kept faithful watch through the years, pronounced the only benediction in its power to give. It struck twelve noon.

Simon again made the trip to Paris for the opening of Louis's will. For his mother, who had saved so carefully for him, he had made provision for a yearly income. Other funds were divided equally between Catherine's and Marie's children. To Simon, went the land at Coupvray. To his friends at the school, his bank account, piano and cello, furniture and books. There were ten other bequests, among them gifts to the church at Coupvray, to the Society for the Blind, his young guide, the infirmary boy, the night watchman, and the housekeeper.

While sorting his possessions friends came across The Box with a note attached, "To be burned without opening." Curious, they opened it and found within the rolls of paper signed by Pierre and other students. It was evident Louis did not want the loans collected. The box and its contents were burned.

Outside the circle of friends in Coupvray and the Institution for Blind Youth in Paris, the passing of Louis Braille went unnoticed. The newspapers of Paris, dated January 6, 1852, told of things political and social but no mention was made of the death of the blind teacher. No one as yet realized the greatness of his work, the enormity of his gift to those handicapped by blindness.

Never again would a small sightless boy weep because there were no books for him to read, nor a young blind man search in vain for learning. Through his six-dot alphabet, Louis Braille, the blind boy of Coupvray had given to those who must read by touch the key to education and equality in a sighted world.

CHAPTER

12

Monuments and Fame

THE YEAR FOLLOWING Louis Braille's death, teachers and students of the Royal Institution for Blind Youth held a commemorative service, May 25, 1853, in his honor. Hippolyte Coltat read his *Notice Biographique sur L. Braille.* A marble bust, with the words *Le Professeur*, etched on its base, was unveiled in the school's vestibule.

Students crowded forward to view the marble likeness with sensitive fingers. The only criticism of the sculptor's work was concerning the rumpled condition of the hair. Hippolyte wrote that Louis was "very careful and *propre*" about his personal appearance.

The six-dot alphabet, known as *Braille* after its inventor, began to make its difficult way outside of

France. Its first introduction into other languages (Latin, Italian, Spanish, German, and English) was by way of the Lord's Prayer. Firm pages of paper were divided by a vertical line. On the left the prayer was embossed in the language of the country, on the right in the corresponding Braille.

Instructors in other countries began to take note of the new system used in France. Conventions were held, demonstrations given. Thirty-five years after Louis's death, almost all the schools for the blind in Europe had adopted the six-dot alphabet. A monument was erected, 1887, on the village square of Coupvray, its height crowned with the bust of the professor. Pictured in bronze is Louis, as teacher, helping a young blind boy read a page of embossed dot-writing. On the stone base are the words, *A Braille, les Aveugles Reconnaissants* (To Braille, the Grateful Blind).

America was one of the slowest countries to adopt Louis Braille's alphabet. Sighted folk, even as Dr. Dafau, stood in the way of the blind.

Instead of using the well-established and tried method of reading and writing for the blind, the United States sought methods of her own. Two new systems for finger readers were adopted, systems as different from each other as Indian sign writing is from

Egyptian picture writing. Blind friends living in separate parts of the country could not read each other's letters, nor could they read the books and papers printed on British presses. Three systems of reading and writing for the English-speaking blind!

The voice of the blind finally made itself heard asking for one, only one, method of reading and writing for English-speaking peoples. A series of tests were given to determine the best of the three systems. The British students won on every score.

More tests—still the British won!

What was this system by which the British blind could outstrip the American blind? None other than Louis Braille's six-dot alphabet, plus contractions peculiar to the English language.

America made the necessary adjustments. At long last the English-speaking blind of the world not only spoke the same language, but wrote it the same way— the Louis Braille way.

One hundred years after his death the fame of the blind French boy had spread over the entire world. France declared a week-long Centennial Celebration in June, 1952. Representatives from twenty different countries participated. The high point of the week was the removal of Louis Braille's body from its humble grave in Coupvray to the Panthéon in the nation's capital, where rest the great and famous of France.

The procession formed at the Royal Institution for Blind Youth. Hundreds of blind, both old and young, from various parts of the world, followed the cortege in a slow-moving procession. The casket was carried up the steps of the Panthéon chapel between a double row of *gardes républicains*, resplendent in uniforms of black, red, and white, their helmets gleaming in the sun. It was borne through the doors over which are the words, "*Aux grands hommes, la patrie reconnaissante.* (To its great men, the country gives honor.)" Most of those who entered could not see the words but their meaning was deeply felt in the man they were honoring.

Many honors have been accorded Louis Braille. Schools, streets, and periodicals have been named for him. He is mentioned in encyclopedias. An issue of stamps (France, January 19, 1948) carries his picture. Monuments have been erected. . . .

But the greatest monuments of all are the numerous libraries for the blind made possible by his six-dot alphabet. The goal of the blind boy of Coupvray has been reached, the goal of "many books" for those who read with seeing fingers.